BECAUSE OF

Bethlehem

BECAUSE OF
Bethlehem

LOVE IS BORN, HOPE IS HERE

STUDY GUIDE
GROUPS / INDIVIDUALS
FOUR SESSIONS

MAX LUCADO

WITH CHRISTINE M. ANDERSON

THOMAS NELSON
Since 1798

Because of Bethlehem Study Guide

© 2016 by Max Lucado

Published in Nashville, Tennessee, by Thomas Nelson. Thomas Nelson is a registered trademark of HarperCollins Christian Publishing, Inc.

Published in association with Anvil II Management, Inc.

Unless otherwise indicated Scripture quotations are taken from the Holy Bible, New International Version®, NIV®. Copyright © 1973, 1978, 1984, 2011 by Biblica, Inc.® Used by permission of Zondervan. All rights reserved worldwide. www.zondervan.com. The "NIV" and "New International Version" are trademarks registered in the United States Patent and Trademark Office by Biblica, Inc.®

Scripture quotations marked MSG are from *The Message*. Copyright © by Eugene H. Peterson 1993, 1994, 1995, 1996, 2000, 2001, 2002. Used by permission of Tyndale House Publishers, Inc.

Scripture quotations marked NCV are taken from the *New Century Version*®. Copyright © 2005 by Thomas Nelson. Used by permission. All rights reserved.

Scripture quotations marked NKJV are taken from the *New King James Version*. Copyright © 1982 by Thomas Nelson, Inc. Used by permission. All rights reserved.

Scripture quotations marked NLT are from the *Holy Bible*, New Living Translation. © 1996, 2004, 2007, 2013 by Tyndale House Foundation. Used by permission of Tyndale House Publishers, Inc., Carol Stream, Illinois 60188. All rights reserved.

Scripture quotations marked NRSV are taken from the *New Revised Standard Version Bible*, copyright © 1989 the Division of Christian Education of the National Council of the Churches of Christ in the United States of America. Used by permission. All rights reserved.

Thomas Nelson titles may be purchased in bulk for educational, business, fundraising, or sales promotional use. For information, please e-mail SpecialMarkets@ThomasNelson.com.

ISBN 978-0-310-68705-4

First Printing July 2016 / Printed in the United States of America

Contents

How to Use This Guide

GROUP SIZE

The *Because of Bethlehem* video study is designed to be experienced in a group setting such as a Bible study, Sunday school class, or any small group gathering. To ensure everyone has enough time to participate in discussions, it is recommended that large groups break up into smaller groups of four to six people each.

MATERIALS NEEDED

Each participant should have his or her own study guide, which includes notes for video segments, directions for activities and discussion questions, as well as practices to deepen learning between sessions.

TIMING

The time notations—for example (16 minutes)—indicate the *actual* time of video segments and the *suggested* times for each activity or discussion. Adhering to the suggested times will enable you to complete each session in about an hour. If you have a longer meeting, you may wish to allow more time for discussion and activities.

PRACTICE

Each session includes an application activity called a practice for group members to complete on their own between meetings. Although the practice is completed outside of group time, it's a good idea to briefly review it before concluding the meeting to clarify any questions and to make sure everyone is on board.

FACILITATION

Each group should appoint a facilitator who is responsible for starting the video and for keeping track of time during discussions and activities. Facilitators may also read questions aloud and monitor discussions, prompting participants to respond and ensuring that everyone has the opportunity to participate.

SESSION 1

God Has a Face

The Word became flesh and blood,
and moved into the neighborhood.
John 1:14 MSG

The celebration of Advent is possible only to
those who are troubled in soul, who know
themselves to be poor and imperfect, and who
look forward to something greater to come.
Dietrich Bonhoeffer,
Dietrich Bonhoeffer's Christmas Sermons

WELCOME

Welcome to session 1 of *Because of Bethlehem*. If this is your first time together as a group, take a moment to introduce yourselves to one another before watching the video. Then let's begin!

VIDEO: *GOD HAS A FACE* (16 MINUTES)

Play the video segment for session 1. As you watch, use the outline provided to follow along or to take additional notes on anything that stands out to you.

Notes

Christmas is a season of traditions. To most kids, that jolly old elf is the very face of Christmas—and that face is everywhere this time of year.

Christmas can also be a season of sadness, of lost hope and disappointments.

The story of Mary and Joseph:

"The Word became flesh and dwelt among us" (John 1:14 NKJV).

Why did God go so far? A chief reason is this: he wants us to know that he gets us.

Through a scandalous pregnancy, an imposed census, an untimely trip, and an overcrowded inn, God triumphed in Mary's story.

The story of George Harley:

Everything changed when the villagers saw the tears of the missionary. Everything changes for us when we see the face of God.

God became one of us, and because of this, he knows us.

If the King was willing to enter the world of animals and shepherds and swaddling clothes, don't you think he's willing to enter yours?

God took on your face in the hope that you would see his.

GROUP DISCUSSION (39 MINUTES)

Take a few minutes with your group members to discuss what you just watched.

1.   What part of the teaching had the most impact on you?

Preparing for Christmas

2. At the beginning of the video, Max acknowledged some of the Christmas traditions he looks forward to each year, such as sleigh bells, carolers, and the holiday classic, *A Charlie Brown Christmas*. These are just a few examples of traditions that typically lead up to Christmas Day and help us experience the Christmas spirit. Using the list of categories below as a prompt, briefly describe one or two traditions that help you to enjoy the season and prepare for Christmas each year.

□ Decorations (decorating home or Christmas tree, going to see the lights, etc.)

□ Christmas cards (sending or receiving)

□ Outdoor activities (snow skiing, ice-skating, snowshoeing, etc.)

□ Food (cooking or eating special meals or desserts)

□ Crafting (making decorations or gifts)

□ Volunteering (serving others through a church or charitable organization)

□ Gift shopping

□ Hosting (parties, special events, overnight guests, etc.)

□ Entertainment (concerts, movies, plays, favorite television shows, etc.)

□ Church (weekly services, special events, etc.)

□ Cultural or ethnic traditions

□ Visit to Santa

□ Family traditions

□ Travel

□ Other: _____

- What do you enjoy most about the tradition you described? How does it contribute to making it feel like Christmas each year?

- What might be gained and what might be lost if you experienced none of these traditions before the day itself? In other words, no holiday decorations, no cards, no special meals or entertainment until Christmas Day. Would you feel more or less prepared to celebrate and enjoy Christmas? Why?

3. For centuries, Christians throughout the world have used the season of Advent to prepare themselves spiritually for Christmas. The word *advent* comes from the Latin word *adventus* and simply means "coming" or "arrival." Beginning each year on the fourth Sunday before Christmas, Advent commemorates the First Advent—Jesus' birth—and also anticipates the Second Advent—Christ's return. Although we tend to think of Advent as a season of celebration, it was originally conceived primarily as a season of preparation—a time for prayer and self-reflection.

- How would you characterize your experience of Advent over the years? For example, is it a tradition you grew up with or is it new to you?

- What, if anything, changes in your perspective when you think of Advent primarily as a season of preparation rather than celebration? Overall, would you say it makes Advent more or less appealing to you? Share the reasons for your response.

God with Us

4. Advent is a season of preparation because it is also a season of *anticipation*—a glorious gift is coming soon and we want to be ready to receive it! In the prologue to his gospel, the apostle John proclaims the miraculous truth of the incarnation, the gift of God with us in human form:

> And the Word became flesh and lived among us, and we have seen his glory, the glory as of a father's only son, full of grace and truth. . . . No one has ever seen God. It is God the only Son, who is close to the Father's heart, who has made him known (John 1:14, 18 NRSV).

Because God became human, we can see and know God in the person of Jesus. We can also rely on the fact that God knows us. He understands how we feel because he has faced what we face, including weakness, testing, and suffering. Author C. S. Lewis elaborates on the vital importance of this truth:

> God could, had he pleased, have been incarnate in a man of iron nerves, the Stoic sort who lets no sigh escape him. Of his great humility he chose to be incarnate in a man of delicate sensibilities who wept at the grave of Lazarus and sweated blood in Gethsemane. . . . He has faced all that the weakest of us face, has shared not only the strength of our nature but every weakness of it except sin. If he had been incarnate in a man of immense natural courage, that would have been for many of us almost the same as his not being incarnate at all.[1]

- Lewis contrasts two options for the kind of man Jesus could have chosen to become—an invincible man of iron nerves, or a vulnerable man of delicate sensibilities. Had Jesus chosen to be the invincible man, how do you imagine it might have undermined the miracle of the incarnation or diminished its power?

- Briefly recall a recent or past experience of weakness, testing, or suffering. As you were going through it, which aspect of Christ's nature would you say you were most aware of and drawn to—his divinity (power) or his humanity (vulnerability)? For example, did you find yourself praying more that Jesus would intervene and change your situation, or that Jesus would be with you and comfort you?

5. Max described the Christmas story as one that actually has particular relevance for those who find themselves in a season of sadness, lost hope, or disappointment. We see this especially in Mary's experience. Although she eagerly anticipated the arrival of her child, nothing leading up to the birth of Jesus would have met Mary's hopes and expectations. She hoped for a joyous celebration with family, but her unwelcome reality was a scandalous pregnancy, an imposed census, an untimely trip, and lowly accommodations with sheep and cattle.

   - As you anticipate these weeks leading up to Christmas, what hopes and expectations are you aware of?

- Words that describe Mary's unwelcome reality include *scandalous*, *imposed*, *untimely*, and *lowly*. What words would you use to describe any unwelcome realities you may be facing this holiday season? Or, in what ways, if any, might this be a difficult time for you?

- In spite of, and out of, Mary's chaos and hardships, Christ came. The season leading up to the first Christmas wasn't what she hoped for, but it was a miracle in the making. At the most unexpected time and place, Mary saw the face of God. Describing how God triumphed in Mary's story Max writes, "The manger dares us to believe the best is yet to be. And it could all begin today." As you consider both your hopes and the unwelcome realities you face, how do you respond to the idea that, like Mary, your circumstances could be a miracle in the making, an occasion in which you may soon see the face of God? What might the manger be daring you to believe?

Walking Together through Advent

6. In addition to studying together, it's also important to walk together through Advent—to share your lives with one another and to be aware of how God is at work among you. In each session, there will be many opportunities to speak life-giving—and life-challenging—words, and to listen to one another deeply.

   As you anticipate the next few weeks of learning and walking together, what request would you like to make of the group? For example, how do you hope other members will challenge you or encourage you? Use one or more of the sentence starters below, or your own statement, to help the group understand the best way to be a good friend to you throughout this study. As each person responds, use the two-page chart that follows to briefly note what is important to that person and how you can be a good friend to him or her during your discussions and times together.

   You can help me to take Advent seriously this year by . . .

   I'd like you to consistently challenge me about . . .

   It really helps me to engage in a group when . . .

   I tend to withdraw or feel anxious when . . .

   In our discussions, the best thing you could do for me is . . .

Name	The Best Way I Can Be a Good Friend to This Person Is . . .

Name	The Best Way I Can Be a Good Friend to This Person Is . . .

INDIVIDUAL ACTIVITY: WHAT I WANT TO REMEMBER (2 MINUTES)

Complete this activity on your own.

1. Briefly review the outline and any notes you took.
2. In the space below, write down the most significant thing you gained in this session—from the teaching, activities, or discussions.

What I want to remember from this session . . .

Advent Practice

Each session in the *Because of Bethlehem* study includes an Advent practice for you to complete between sessions. Although the practice is completed on your own and outside of group time, it's a good idea to briefly preview the practice description before concluding your meeting each week. As an intentional act of preparing our hearts for Christmas, the Advent practices throughout the study require setting aside a brief amount of time each day to complete. To get the most out of the practice, it's important not to hurry or try to complete activities at the last minute.

In addition to the Advent practice, session 1 also includes an optional Advent reflection. This brief exercise is designed to help you begin Advent by considering how the weeks leading up to Christmas typically impact you. It's not necessary to read through the reflection as a group, but before concluding, do review together the session 1 Advent practice, which follows the reflection.

CLOSING PRAYER

Close your time together with prayer.

Advent Reflection and Practice

ADVENT REFLECTION: PREPARE HIM ROOM

"Let every heart prepare him room," writes Isaac Watts in the beloved Christmas hymn "Joy to the World." And that is what Advent is intended to help us do. It is a season of preparation and anticipation, a time to ready our hearts and lives for the arrival of the King. But too often, the time and attention required for spiritual preparation gets lost in the busyness and pressures of the holiday season. Author Ronald Rolheiser writes:

> Our time of preparation is generally more of a time to prepare our houses than a time to prepare our souls, more of a time of shopping than of prayer, and more of a time of already feasting than a time of fasting as a preparation for a feast. Today, Advent is perhaps more about already

celebrating Christmas than it is about preparing for it. And the end result is that, like the biblical innkeepers who had no room for Mary and Joseph at the first Christmas, we generally arrive at Christmas with "no room at the inn," no space in our lives for a spiritual rebirth.[2]

If we want to arrive at Christmas with a heart wide open for the Christ child, we need to be intentional about making room for him now. The question Advent invites us to consider is this: *How ready am I for the arrival of the King?* Before engaging the Advent practice for this week, take a few moments to reflect on what the weeks ahead might be like for you.

1. Use the statements that follow to briefly assess how these weeks leading up to Christmas typically impact you. For each statement, circle the number on the continuum that best describes your response.

> *Physical*: During the weeks leading up to Christmas, I am consistently able to meet my body's needs for rest, exercise, nutrition, hygiene, medical care, etc.
>
> | 1 | 2 | 3 | 4 | 5 | 6 | 7 | 8 | 9 | 10 |
> |---|---|---|---|---|---|---|---|---|---|
> | Not true at all of me | | | | Moderately true of me | | | | Completely true of me | |

Relational: During the weeks leading up to Christmas, I am consistently able to give and receive love, maintain healthy boundaries, be attentive to the needs and concerns of others, and to allow others to care for and listen to me.

1	2	3	4	5	6	7	8	9	10

Not true
at all of me

Moderately
true of me

Completely
true of me

Emotional: During the weeks leading up to Christmas, I am consistently able to express feelings, manage stress, and maintain perspective when things don't go my way.

1	2	3	4	5	6	7	8	9	10

Not true
at all of me

Moderately
true of me

Completely
true of me

Pace of life: During the weeks leading up to Christmas, I am consistently able to maintain a reasonable pace of life. I have adequate time to accomplish tasks, sufficient margins to be flexible with changing demands, and time to enjoy people and activities that give me life.

1	2	3	4	5	6	7	8	9	10

Not true
at all of me

Moderately
true of me

Completely
true of me

Financial: During the weeks leading up to Christmas, I am consistently able to avoid debt, be intentional with spending, generous in giving, and wise in saving.

1	2	3	4	5	6	7	8	9	10

Not true
at all of me

Moderately
true of me

Completely
true of me

Spiritual: During the weeks leading up to Christmas, I am consistently able to rest in God, spend time with him, respond to his leading, trust him with unknowns, grow in my love for him, receive love from him, etc.

1	2	3	4	5	6	7	8	9	10

Not true at all of me				Moderately true of me				Completely true of me

- Which of the six areas of life, if any, tend to suffer or be diminished during the weeks leading up to Christmas? Which, if any, tend to thrive or be strengthened?

- Consider the impact these weeks typically have on your ability to prepare yourself spiritually for Christmas. In what ways is this season your *ally*, a partner that helps you to draw closer to God and others?

- In what ways is this season your *adversary*, an opponent that makes it harder for you to draw closer to God and others?

2. Author Ronald Rolheiser says we often arrive at Christmas unprepared, "with 'no room in the inn,' no space in our lives for spiritual rebirth." As you reflect on your responses to question 1, what kinds of things would you say have the greatest potential to crowd your heart and life in the weeks ahead? Specifically, what might you have to let go of in order to make space for Christ, to prepare him room?

Expectations—of myself and others—I might have to let go of . . .

Plans/commitments I might have to let go of . . .

Tasks I might have to let go of . . .

Spending I might have to let go of . . .

Hurts I might have to let go of . . .

Habits I might have to let go of . . .

Other things I might have to let go of . . .

3. What comes to mind when you consider the Advent question: How ready am I for *the arrival of the King?*

ADVENT PRACTICE: PREPARE HIM ROOM

The practice for this week is to increase your awareness of the ways you might be making or not making room for Christ in your everyday choices. To be aware of something is to be attentive to it—to listen, watch, and observe. Awareness also requires being respectful and gracious, which means observing without making judgments and without guilt trips. The invitation of this practice is to set aside time to simply notice and then to reflect on what you see.

1. Set aside fifteen minutes at the beginning or end of five days this week to do a "room" review—to notice the ways you are or are not making room for Christ. Just as a coach and athletes sometimes watch game-day videos to see what worked and what needs more practice, imagine you and Jesus together are watching a video replay of the previous twenty-four hours.

2. Divide your day into three parts: morning, afternoon, and evening. As you reflect on each part of the day, prayerfully consider two questions:

    > Lord, *in what ways did I make room for you in my life or in my heart?*
    > Lord, *in what ways did I fail to make room for you in my life or in my heart?*

    We make room for Christ when we choose him and welcome him into every moment, no matter how small. We fail to make room for Christ when we choose something else over him, or when he is not made welcome in any way. Here are some examples of small ways we might welcome or not welcome Christ into our lives and into our hearts:

- We can choose to limit commitments in order to get adequate sleep and avoid feeling frantic or run down, or choose not to limit commitments.
- We can choose to set aside the to-do list in order to be with and enjoy another person, or choose not to set aside the to-do list.
- We can choose to believe the best when we could dwell instead on the worst, or choose not to believe the best.
- We can choose to trust God and surrender rather than manipulate and control, or choose not to trust God and surrender.

3. As you and Jesus together reflect on the day, use the space provided below or a journal to write down at least two or three observations about what you notice. (If you find it challenging to make these observations after the fact, consider keeping a pad of paper with you and writing down your observations as they happen throughout the day.) Then prayerfully surrender what you've written, inviting Jesus to help you make room for him and welcome him in the day ahead.

4. At the end of the week, review your daily observations. What stands out most to you about the ways in which you routinely make room or fail to make room for Christ? Write your observations in the space provided or in a journal.

5. Bring your notes to the next group gathering. You'll have a chance to talk about your experiences and observations at the beginning of the session 2 discussion.

Day 1 Room Review

Day 2 Room Review

Day 3 Room Review

Day 4 Room Review

Day 5 Room Review

Week in Review

Briefly review your daily observations. What stands out most to you about the ways in which you routinely make room or fail to make room for Christ?

Worship Works Wonders

Oh, how my soul praises the Lord. How
my spirit rejoices in God my Savior! . . .
For the Mighty One is holy, and he
has done great things for me.
Mary, the mother of Jesus
(Luke 1:46–47, 49 NLT)

Worship is the single most powerful
force in completing and sustaining
restoration in the whole person.
Dallas Willard, Renovation of the Heart

GROUP DISCUSSION: CHECKING IN (8 MINUTES)

A key part of getting to know God better is sharing your journey with others. Before watching the video, take some time to briefly check in with one another about your experiences since the last session. For example:

- Briefly share your experience of the session 1 practice, "Prepare Him Room." The focus of this practice was to increase awareness of the ways in which you make room or fail to make room for Christ in your everyday choices. In what ways did this practice challenge you? In what ways did it encourage you?
- What did you notice about the ways in which you routinely make room or fail to make room for Christ in your everyday life?
- How did the previous session impact your daily life or your relationship with God?
- What questions would you like to ask the other members of your group?

VIDEO: *WORSHIP WORKS WONDERS* (17 MINUTES)

Play the video segment for session 2. As you watch, use the outline provided to follow along or to take additional notes on anything that stands out to you.

Notes

We all worship something. The time we spend worshiping the *wrong* thing is time we never get back to worship the *right* thing.

Christmas and gift giving have always been associated with each other:

The angels gave Jesus the gift of worship.

God is on the lookout for those who will choose to worship him.

Anytime we trust an object or activity to give us life and meaning, we worship it. When we make good things our ultimate things, we set ourselves up for disappointment.

To worship substitutes for God is to be satisfied, then brokenhearted; infatuated, then discouraged; enthralled, then angry. Worship does to the soul what a spring rain does to a thirsty field. It soaks down, seeps in, and stirs life.

How to make a big deal about the arrival of the King:

Worship verbally. Christ tells us it is "out of the abundance of the heart that the mouth speaks" (Matthew 12:34 NKJV). If you love God, let him know.

Worship in community. "Let's see how inventive we can be in encouraging love and helping out, not avoiding worshiping together as some do but spurring each other on" (Hebrews 10:24–25 MSG).

Worship demonstrably. Let your body express what your heart is feeling.

Don't miss out on the opportunity to give God worship.

"Here I am!" Jesus invites. "I stand at the door and knock. If you hear my voice and open the door, I will come in and eat with you, and you will eat with me" (Revelation 3:20 NCV).

He is gentle and polite. He never forces his way in. He never demands to meet with us for fellowship.

Even if you've turned Christ away before, you can still don the robe of grace, soar on wings of faith, take your place in the heavenly chorus, and sing, "Glory to God in the highest."

GROUP DISCUSSION (33 MINUTES)

Take a few minutes with your group members to discuss what you just watched.

1. What part of the teaching had the most impact on you?

We All Worship Something

2. Max said that whether we are eight or eighty, we all worship something. When he was eight, the object of his love and adoration was a bike he wanted for Christmas. He wrote letters to Santa describing not only the details of what he wanted—a Schwinn with a banana seat and monkey handlebars—but also how it would make him the "happiest and most appreciative boy in town."

    • When you think back to your childhood or teen years, what would you say was your "bike" equivalent— something you obsessed about and desired with all your heart? As part of your response, share any details you can recall that were especially important to you.

    • Eight-year-old Max imagined that the bike would not only change his life, but that it would also change *him*—he would become supremely happy and appreciative. How did your younger self imagine life would be different if you had what you wanted most? In what ways, if any, did you expect it to change not just your life but *you*?

3. Like Max's bike, the things we set our hearts on typically aren't bad things but good things that have the potential to become ultimate things. Listed below are several categories of good things we might enjoy in life. Briefly review the list, placing a check mark next to the top two or three that are primary sources of happiness, meaning, security, or identity for you right now.

☐ *Achievement/success* (education, sports, hobbies, career, etc.)

☐ *Power/influence* (control, authority, confidence, etc.)

☐ *Belonging/affirmation* (peer acceptance/approval, reputation, social media status, etc.)

☐ *Lifestyle* (time and resources devoted to pursuing leisure, comfort, entertainment, etc.)

☐ *Religion* (beliefs, faith community, spiritual practices, etc.)

☐ *Appearance* (grooming, clothing, jewelry, body size/shape, etc.)

☐ *Finances* (earning, giving, saving, spending, debt, etc.)

☐ *Possessions* (house/property, furniture, vehicle, investment portfolio, electronics/gadgets, etc.)

☐ *Family* (spouse, children, parents, etc.)

☐ *Health* (sleep, exercise, weight, medical care, etc.)

☐ Other: _____

- Share one of the categories you checked. What makes this area of life especially significant to you right now? In what ways is it a good gift from God—a source of happiness, meaning, security, or identity?

- When we make a good thing an ultimate thing— something we set our hearts on above all else—we set ourselves up for disappointment. Max said it is to be "satisfied, then brokenhearted; infatuated, then discouraged; enthralled, then angry." In what ways, if any, have you experienced this dynamic in connection with the good gift you just described? How has it diminished or failed to provide happiness, meaning, protection, or self-worth?

- What parallels might there be between the area of life you described and your relationship with God? In other words, how might the goodness this gift provides also point to something you need from God, find it difficult to entrust to God, or are learning from God?

The Power of Worship

4. When good things become ultimate things—substitute gods—the challenge we face is this: How can we set our hearts on God above all else without discarding or doing damage to the good things we love? The answer: we immerse ourselves in heartfelt worship. Author and pastor Timothy Keller describes it this way:

> If we have made idols out of work and family, we do not want to stop loving our work and our family. Rather, we want to love Christ so much *more* that we are not enslaved by our attachments. . . . "Rejoicing" is a way of praising God until the heart is sweetened and rested, and until it relaxes its grip on anything else it thinks that it needs.[3]

- How would you describe what it means in practical terms to be enslaved by attachments—to have a tight grip on whatever it is we think we need most? Consider how a tight grip might shape things like everyday choices, relationships, personal growth, etc.

- What does the image of a relaxed grip suggest about what it means to love God *more*?

- Keller uses the words *sweetened*, *rested*, and *relaxed* to describe the heart transformed by worship. Which of these words comes closest to describing a transformation you would like to experience during Advent?

5. The angels in the Christmas story rejoiced in worship when they proclaimed to the shepherds, "Glory to God in the highest heaven, and on earth peace to those on whom his favor rests" (Luke 2:14). Max described three ways we can join with the angels in praise and adoration: we can worship *verbally*, worship *in community*, and worship *demonstrably*. As part of this group meeting, you have an opportunity to practice all three.

   On the following pages is Psalm 103, a hymn of praise and adoration composed by King David. Use the psalm to worship *verbally* and *in community* by reading it together responsively. As you read, allow the words of the psalmist to be your words, expressing your heart of love and gratitude to God. Worship *demonstrably* by first standing together in a circle. Then, if a word or phrase is especially meaningful to you, allow your body to express what your heart is feeling— raise a hand or open palm, sway in rhythm to the words, or respond in any other way that expresses your heart for God.

   Appoint one person to read the lines designated "leader." As you read the psalm, pay attention to words or phrases that stand out to you for any reason. After reading the psalm, use the questions that follow to continue your discussion.

- What words or phrases from the psalm stood out to you? Share the reasons for your response.
- What, if anything, shifted in your heart as you read the psalm together? For example, was your heart able to relax its grip, to sweeten to God, to rest?

PSALM 103

Leader:

> Praise the LORD, my soul;
> > all my inmost being, praise his holy name.

Group:

> Praise the LORD, my soul,
> > and forget not all his benefits—
> who forgives all your sins
> > and heals all your diseases,
> who redeems your life from the pit
> > and crowns you with love and compassion,
> who satisfies your desires with good things
> > so that your youth is renewed like the eagle's.

Leader:

> The LORD works righteousness
> > and justice for all the oppressed.
> He made known his ways to Moses,
> > his deeds to the people of Israel.

(cont.)

Group:

> The LORD is compassionate and gracious,
>> slow to anger, abounding in love.
> He will not always accuse,
>> nor will he harbor his anger forever;
> he does not treat us as our sins deserve
>> or repay us according to our iniquities.
> For as high as the heavens are above the earth,
>> so great is his love for those who fear him;
> as far as the east is from the west,
>> so far has he removed our transgressions from us.

Leader:

> As a father has compassion on his children,
>> so the LORD has compassion on those who fear him;
> for he knows how we are formed,
>> he remembers that we are dust.

Group:

> The life of mortals is like grass,
>> they flourish like a flower of the field;
> the wind blows over it and it is gone,
>> and its place remembers it no more.
> But from everlasting to everlasting
>> the LORD's love is with those who fear him,
>> and his righteousness with their children's
>> children—
> with those who keep his covenant
>> and remember to obey his precepts.

Leader:

> The LORD has established his throne in heaven,
>> and his kingdom rules over all.

All:

> Praise the LORD, you his angels,
>> you mighty ones who do his bidding,
>> who obey his word.
> Praise the LORD, all his heavenly hosts,
>> you his servants who do his will.
> Praise the LORD, all his works
>> everywhere in his dominion.
> Praise the LORD, my soul.

Walking Together through Advent

6. At the end of the session 1 group discussion, you had the opportunity to make a request of the group and to write down the best ways you could be good friends to one another.

   - Briefly restate what you asked for from the group in session 1. What additions or clarifications would you like to make that would help the group to know more about how to be a good friend to you? As each person responds, add any additional information to the session 1 chart. (If you were absent from the last session, share your response to session 1, question 6. Then use the chart to write down what is important to each member of the group.)

- In what ways, if any, did you find yourself responding differently to other members of the group in this session based on what they asked for in the previous session? What made that easy or difficult for you to do?

INDIVIDUAL ACTIVITY: WHAT I WANT TO REMEMBER (2 MINUTES)

Complete this activity on your own.

1. Briefly review the outline and any notes you took.
2. In the space below, write down the most significant thing you gained in this session—from the teaching, activities, or discussions.

   What I want to remember from this session . . .

ADVENT PRACTICE

Before concluding, briefly preview the session 2 Advent practice, "Worship and Respond."

CLOSING PRAYER

Close your time together with prayer.

Advent Practice

WORSHIP AND RESPOND

In the group session, Max taught that worship is powerful—it can change our lives and the lives of others. This connection between worship and transformation is one the apostle Paul emphasized in his letter to the church at Rome:

> And so, dear brothers and sisters, I plead with you to give your bodies to God because of all he has done for you. Let them be a living and holy sacrifice—the kind he will find acceptable. This is truly the way to worship him. Don't copy the behavior and customs of this world, but let God transform you into a new person by changing the way you think. Then you will learn to know God's will for you, which is good and pleasing and perfect (Romans 12:1-2 NLT).

For a fresh perspective on this familiar passage, read it again from *The Message*:

> So here's what I want you to do, God helping you: Take your everyday, ordinary life—your sleeping, eating, going-to-work, and walking-around life—and place it before God as an offering. Embracing what God does for you is the best thing you can do for him. Don't become so well-adjusted to your culture that you fit into it without even thinking. Instead, fix your attention on God. You'll be changed from the inside out. Readily recognize what he wants from you, and quickly respond to it. Unlike the culture around you, always dragging you down to its level of immaturity, God brings the best out of you, develops well-formed maturity in you (Romans 12:1-2 MSG).

This week, you'll build on the session 1 Advent practice by using everyday acts of worship to continue preparing room for Christ in your life and in your heart.

1. Use the events, tasks, and interactions of the day as prompts for worship. A trip to the grocery store, paying bills, writing an email, feeding a small child, talking with a friend or colleague—every moment can become an occasion for worship. In those moments, make worship practical by following the three actions described in the Romans passage: *(1) fix your attention on God, (2) recognize what he wants from you, and then (3) quickly respond to it.* If you find it helpful, write the three actions on a Post-it note and place it where you will see it often. Or, make the actions an alert on your

phone, watch, or laptop as a daily reminder to worship in that moment.

2. At the beginning or end of five days this week, set aside fifteen minutes for prayerful reflection.
   - Begin with a minute or two of silence, asking God to quiet your mind and your heart.
   - As you reflect on the previous twenty-four hours, prayerfully consider your experiences with everyday acts of worship:

     What happened when I chose to fix my attention on God, recognize what he wanted from me, and then quickly respond to it?
     What happened when I chose not to?

     Use the space provided below or a journal to write down two or three observations.

3. Close your time by placing yourself and the day ahead before God as an offering. Surrender any events, relationships, or other attachments you are holding with a "tight grip" (see question 4 in the group session). If you find it helpful, use the prayer of the psalmist, "Oh LORD, I give my life to you. I trust in you, my God!" (Psalm 25:1–2 NLT).

4. At the end of the week, review your daily observations. Focus on the connection between worship and change described by the apostle Paul (see Romans 12:1–2). What, if anything, changed in you or in your behavior through your daily acts of worship? How did God use these moments of everyday worship to bring the best out in you? Write your observations in the space provided or in a journal.

5. Bring your notes to the next group gathering. You'll have a chance to talk about your experiences and observations at the beginning of the session 3 discussion.

Day 1 Worship Review

Day 2 Worship Review

Day 3 Worship Review

Day 4 Worship Review

Day 5 Worship Review

Week in Review

Briefly review your daily observations. What, if anything, changed in you or in your behavior through your daily acts of worship? How did God use these moments of everyday worship to bring the best out of you?

God Guides the Wise

The star they had seen in the east
guided them to Bethlehem. It went ahead
of them and stopped over the place
where the child was. When they saw
the star, they were filled with joy!
Matthew 2:9–10 NLT

The wise men see new life as a
promise and they bless it; Herod sees
new life as threat and curses it.
Ronald Rolheiser,
"King Herod and the Wise Men"

GROUP DISCUSSION: CHECKING IN (8 MINUTES)

A key part of getting to know God better is sharing your journey with others. Before watching the video, take some time to briefly check in with one another about your experiences since the last session. For example:

- Briefly share your experience of the session 2 practice, "Worship and Respond." The focus of the practice was to engage in everyday worship by taking three actions: *Fix your attention on God, recognize what he wants from you, and then quickly respond to it.* Which of the three actions did you find easiest or hardest to follow through on? Why?
- What, if anything, changed in you or in your behavior through your daily acts of worship? How did God use these moments of everyday worship to bring the best out of you?
- How did the previous session impact your daily life or your relationship with God?
- What questions would you like to ask the other members of your group?

VIDEO: *GOD GUIDES THE WISE* (14 MINUTES)

Play the video segment for session 3. As you watch, use the outline provided to follow along or to take additional notes on anything that stands out to you.

Notes

If we truly desire to experience all that God has to offer, we need to step out of our plan, step into his, and travel the magi road.

The magi's story is our story. We're all travelers in need of direction. God gives it. The story of the wise men shows us how.

God used the natural world to get the magi's attention. "We have seen his star in the east" (Matthew 2:2 NKJV).

"The basic reality of God is plain enough. Open your eyes and there it is! By taking a long and thoughtful look at what God has created, people have always been able to see what their eyes as such can't see: eternal power, for instance, and the mystery of his divine being" (Romans 1:19–20 MSG).

Unlike Herod, the wise men followed God's leading.

Herod and the magi share the same chapter but not the same heart. Herod's example shows us that believing is not obedience, and pride can blind us even when we know the truth.

The ultimate aim of all God's messages, both miraculous and written, is to shed the light of heaven on Jesus. The magi found the Christ because they heeded the sign and believed the Scripture.

> Unlike the scholars of the Torah, the wise men read the prophecy and responded to it. The hearts of the wise men were open to God's gifts.

As with the wise men, God uses every possible means to communicate with us. He wants to help us find our way home.

Christmas celebrates God breaking through to our world. He is the pursuer, the teacher, and won't leave us in the dark. He sends signals and messages: Hope. Life. Love.

When God sends the signs, may you be wise and allow them to lead you to Scripture. As Scripture directs, may you be humble. As you are humble, may it lead you to worship.

GROUP DISCUSSION (36 MINUTES)

Take a few minutes with your group members to discuss what you just watched.

1. What part of the teaching had the most impact on you?

A Good Road Trip

2. Ever since the magi first went in search of Jesus more than two thousand years ago, it seems that Christmas and "road trip" have gone together. Whether it's during the holidays

or at any other time, what makes a good road trip for you? Briefly review the list below and place a check mark next to the statement that best describes your response.

It's only a good road trip if . . .

☐ I can anticipate needs and keep everyone happy and content.

☐ I succeed in getting there faster than ever and/or with better gas mileage.

☐ I can see something unique or beautiful along the way.

☐ I can have some quiet to think my own thoughts, and some conversation to talk about ideas that interest me.

☐ I feel assured that everybody knows and will follow the rules.

☐ I'm with fun people and we have exciting things to do and see.

☐ I can defy the speed limit without getting caught.

☐ I can keep the atmosphere relaxed and smooth over any conflicts.

☐ I can keep everybody in line and on schedule so things go the way I think they should.

☐ Other: _____

- Share the statement you checked. Why is this important for a good road trip? To illustrate your response, share any stories from previous road trips that come to mind.

- What similarities might there be, if any, between how you approach a road trip and how you approach your life overall? Or, is there another statement on the list that comes closer to describing how you approach your life overall? Share the reasons for your response.

Signs and Wisdom

3. Max made a connection between how the magi approached their journey and what it means to be wise in the way we approach our lives. "Their story is our story," he said. "We're all travelers in need of direction, and God gives it. The magi show us how to respond with wisdom."

   Beginning below, read together the full story of the magi's journey recorded in Matthew 2:1–12. Go around the group and have each person read aloud two or three verses at a time. As the story is read, pay particular attention to the differences in how Herod, the priests/teachers, and the magi respond to signs that point to the Messiah.

   [1] After Jesus was born in Bethlehem in Judea, during the time of King Herod, Magi from the east came to Jerusalem [2] and asked, "Where is the one who has been born king of the Jews? We saw his star when it rose and have come to worship him."

   [3] When King Herod heard this he was disturbed, and all Jerusalem with him. [4] When he had called

together all the people's chief priests and teachers of the law, he asked them where the Messiah was to be born. ⁵ "In Bethlehem in Judea," they replied, "for this is what the prophet has written:

> ⁶ "'But you, Bethlehem, in the land of Judah,
> are by no means least among the rulers of Judah;
> for out of you will come a ruler
> who will shepherd my people Israel.'" [Micah 5:2, 4]

⁷ Then Herod called the Magi secretly and found out from them the exact time the star had appeared. ⁸ He sent them to Bethlehem and said, "Go and search carefully for the child. As soon as you find him, report to me, so that I too may go and worship him."

⁹ After they had heard the king, they went on their way, and the star they had seen when it rose went ahead of them until it stopped over the place where the child was. ¹⁰ When they saw the star, they were overjoyed. ¹¹ On coming to the house, they saw the child with his mother Mary, and they bowed down and worshiped him. Then they opened their treasures and presented him with gifts of gold, frankincense and myrrh. ¹² And having been warned in a dream not to go back to Herod, they returned to their country by another route (Matthew 2:1-12).

All three characters—Herod, the priests/teachers, and the magi—not only had access to the same signs from God, but all three also appear to have believed the Micah prophecy. Herod took it seriously enough to defy it; the priests/

teachers knew it chapter and verse but did nothing; and the
magi committed themselves to following it.

- Given that all three had access to the same signs and
  shared the same belief, what accounts for the radical
  differences in their responses? In other words, why might
  news of the Messiah make Herod defiant, the priests/
  teachers complacent, and the magi joyful?

- Max said that the ultimate aim of all God's messages is
  to shed the light of heaven on Jesus. The magi never had
  a complete road map to Jesus, but at each point along
  their journey, they kept moving toward the light they
  had. What kinds of things did responding with wisdom
  require of the magi? What does their example suggest
  about what it means to navigate our own lives with
  wisdom?

4. To better understand the demonstrations of wisdom (and
   lack of wisdom) in the magi story, read aloud the following
   passage in which the apostle James contrasts two kinds of
   wisdom. As you read, underline any words or phrases that
   stand out to you in connection with King Herod, the priests/
   teachers, and the magi.

If you are wise and understand God's ways, prove it by living an honorable life, doing good works with the humility that comes from wisdom. But if you are bitterly jealous and there is selfish ambition in your heart, don't cover up the truth with boasting and lying. For jealousy and selfishness are not God's kind of wisdom. Such things are earthly, unspiritual, and demonic. For wherever there is jealousy and selfish ambition, there you will find disorder and evil of every kind.

But the wisdom from above is first of all pure. It is also peace loving, gentle at all times, and willing to yield to others. It is full of mercy and the fruit of good deeds. It shows no favoritism and is always sincere. And those who are peacemakers will plant seeds of peace and reap a harvest of righteousness (James 3:13–18 NLT).

- What parallels do you recognize between this passage and the magi story? Specifically, how do Herod and the priests/teachers illustrate earthly, unspiritual wisdom? How do the magi illustrate wisdom from above?

- James uses vivid words and phrases to describe wisdom from below and wisdom from above. To gain deeper insights into both kinds of wisdom, work through the passage and consider the opposites of the words and phrases he uses. For example, to better understand wisdom from below, describe the opposites of words like *pure, peace loving, gentle at all times*, etc. To better understand wisdom from above, describe the opposites of words like *jealousy, selfish ambition, disorder*, etc.

- What does James' teaching—and considering the opposites—reveal about what godly wisdom looks like in everyday life?

Walking Together through Advent

5. Christmas celebrates God breaking through to our world. He is the pursuer, the teacher, and he doesn't leave us in the dark. He uses Scripture, the natural world, and our personal experiences with him to send us signals and messages: *Hope. Life. Love.* As you continue to journey through Advent to Christmas, what word or phrase would you use to describe the message you most need to hear from God right now? Or, how do you hope he might shed the light of heaven on your path?

INDIVIDUAL ACTIVITY: WHAT I WANT TO REMEMBER (2 MINUTES)

Complete this activity on your own.

1. Briefly review the outline and any notes you took.
2. In the space below, write down the most significant thing you gained in this session—from the teaching, activities, or discussions.

What I want to remember from this session . . .

ADVENT PRACTICE

Before concluding, briefly preview the session 3 Advent practice, "Seek the Light of Christ."

CLOSING PRAYER

Close your time together with prayer.

Get a Head Start on the
Session 4 Discussion

As part of the group discussion for session 4, you'll have an opportunity to talk about what you've learned and experienced together throughout the *Because of Bethlehem* study. Between now and your next meeting, take a few moments to review the previous sessions and identify the teaching, discussions, or practices that stand out most to you. Use the worksheet on the following pages to briefly summarize the highlights of what you've learned and experienced.

HEAD START WORKSHEET

Take a few moments to reflect on what you've learned and experienced throughout the *Because of Bethlehem* study. You may want to review notes from the video teaching, what you wrote down for "What I Want to Remember" at the end of each group session, and observations from weekly practice notes. Here are some questions you might consider as part of your review:

- What insights did I gain from this session?
- What was the most important thing I learned about myself in this session?
- How did this session help me to prepare my heart for Christmas?
- How did I experience God's presence or leading related to this session?
- How did this session impact my relationships with the other people in the group?

Use the spaces provided below and on the next page to briefly summarize what you've learned and experienced for each session.

Session 1: God Has a Face

Session 2: Worship Works Wonders

Session 3: God Guides the Wise

Advent Practice

SEEK THE LIGHT OF CHRIST

Light is one of the most prominent themes and images of Advent. Speaking of the promised Messiah, the prophet Isaiah wrote, "The people who walk in darkness will see a great light" (Isaiah 9:2 NLT). The apostle John wrote of Jesus' arrival on earth, "The true light that gives light to everyone was coming into the world" (John 1:9). And Jesus later said of himself, "I am the light of the world. If you follow me, you won't have to walk in darkness, because you will have the light that leads to life" (John 8:12 NLT). Like the magi of old who first traveled through darkness by the light of a God-sent star, Advent invites us to seek and follow the light God gives as we journey to Christmas. New Testament scholar N. T. Wright describes why this is so important:

> Christmas is not a reminder that the world is really quite a
> nice old place. It reminds us that the world is a shockingly

bad old place, where wickedness flourishes unchecked. . . .
Christmas is God lighting a candle; and you don't light a
candle in a room that's already full of sunlight. You light
a candle in a room that's so murky that the candle, when
lit, reveals just how bad things really are. The light shines
in the darkness, says St. John, and the darkness has not
overcome it. . . . Christmas is the reality, which shows up
the rest of "reality."[4]

The magi never had a complete road map to Jesus, but at each
point along their journey, they kept moving toward the light they
had. "Hope in the LORD *and keep his way*," writes the psalmist
(Psalm 37:34, emphasis added). This is what it means to navigate
dark seasons with wisdom—we keep moving toward the light
we have even as we seek the greater light we long for. This week,
you'll continue to prepare your heart for Christmas—to make
him room—by seeking the light of Christ.

1. Identify one area of life in which you are walking in darkness. For example, it might be a challenging circumstance, a
   personal struggle, or a difficult relationship. Allow this to be
   your focus for seeking the light of Christ this week.

2. Identify the light you have in this situation—the one or two
   ways you already know God wants you to hope in him and
   keep his way. Or, read Psalm 37, a psalm of wisdom and
   practical instruction. Choose one truth you resonate with to
   be the light you follow this week. For example:

   • "Trust in the LORD and do good." (v. 3)
   • "Take delight in the LORD." (v. 4)

- "Commit your way to the LORD." (v. 5)
- "Be still before the LORD and wait patiently for him." (v. 7)
- "Do not fret." (vv. 7, 8)

3. Train your heart to seek the light of Christ by training your eyes to notice all the lights that surround you—everything from sunrise to holiday lights to the little light at the back of the refrigerator. Stuck in rush-hour traffic? Let the brake lights on the car in front of you be the prompt that reminds you to follow the light you have:

    - *Even in my darkness, I will trust in the Lord and do good.*
    - *Even in my darkness, I will take delight in the Lord.*
    - *Even in my darkness, I will commit my way to the Lord.*
    - *Even in my darkness, I will be still before the Lord and wait patiently for him.*
    - *Even in my darkness, I will not fret.*

    If you find it helpful, keep a daily light list or use your smartphone to take a picture of all the lights that prompt you to invite the light of Christ into each moment of your day. Write your light statement on a Post-it note and place it where you will see it often. Or use a visual reminder such as an image of a star or a lit candle as the wallpaper on your phone or laptop.

4. Set aside fifteen minutes at the beginning or end of five days this week for prayerful reflection.

    - Begin with a minute or two of silence, asking God to quiet your mind and your heart.

- As you reflect on the previous twenty-four hours, prayerfully consider your experiences with training your heart to seek the light of Christ in the darkness you identified.

> *What is the light I already have in my darkness—the truth I can rely on and follow?*
>
> *When did I follow this light? When did I fail to follow it?*
>
> *What new light, if any, do I sense God inviting me to follow?*

Use the space provided on the following pages or a journal to write down two or three observations.

- Close your time by surrendering your concerns to the God who "reveals deep and mysterious things and knows what lies hidden in darkness, though he is surrounded by light" (Daniel 2:22 NLT). Ask for whatever it is you need from God to keep following the light you have.

- At the end of the week, review your daily observations. What did following the light you have require of you? In what ways, if any, did it help you? For example, to experience hope, to make wise decisions, to find greater light in your darkness? Write your observations in the space provided or in a journal.

- Bring your notes to the next group gathering. You'll have a chance to talk about your experiences and observations at the beginning of the session 4 discussion.

Day 1 Light Review

Day 2 Light Review

Day 3 Light Review

Day 4 Light Review

Day 5 Light Review

Week in Review

Briefly review your daily observations. What did following the light you have require of you? In what ways, if any, did it help you? For example, to experience hope, to make wise decisions, to find greater light in your darkness?

Every Heart a Manger

For this is how God loved the world:
He gave his one and only Son, so that
everyone who believes in him will
not perish but have eternal life.
John 3:16 NLT

God didn't stay at a distance. . . .
He took us seriously enough to come
into our world as one of us.
N. T. Wright,
For All God's Worth

GROUP DISCUSSION: CHECKING IN (8 MINUTES)

A key part of getting to know God better is sharing your journey with others. Before watching the video, take some time to briefly check in with one another about your experiences since the last session. For example:

- Briefly share your experience of the session 3 practice, "Seek the Light of Christ." The focus of this practice was to use all the lights that surround you as prompts to seek the light of Christ. What about this exercise most surprised you?
- What did following the light you have require of you? In what ways, if any, did it help you? For example, to experience hope, to make wise decisions, to find greater light in your darkness?
- What insights did you discover in the personal study or in the chapters you read from the book *Because of Bethlehem*?
- How did the previous session impact your daily life or your relationship with God?
- What questions would you like to ask the other members of your group?

VIDEO: *EVERY HEART A MANGER* (16 MINUTES)

Play the video segment for session 4. As you watch, use the outline provided to follow along or to take additional notes on anything that stands out to you.

Notes

The story of Christmas is the story of God's relentless love for us. We might question his actions, decisions, or declarations. But because of Bethlehem, we can never question his unquenchable affection for us.

If he is willing to be born in a barnyard, expect him to be at work anywhere. No place is too common. No person is too hardened. No distance is too far. There is no limit to his love.

Jesus' time on earth would be a search-and-rescue mission.

In the manger God loves you, and through the cross he saves you. But has he taken you to his home? Not yet. He has work for you to do. He wants the world to see what God can do with his purchased possessions.

God prunes us.

God "decorates" us. He festoons us with the fruit of the Spirit. He crowns us. He sends his angels to protect us and his Word as a star to guide us.

God surrounds us with his grace. We become the distribution point of God's gifts.

God places us. "You made my whole being; you formed me in my mother's body. I praise you because you made me in an amazing and wonderful way. What you have done is wonderful. . . . All the days planned for me were written in your book before I was one day old" (Psalm 139:13–14, 16 NCV).

Christmas invites us to believe the wildest of promises: God became one of us so we could become one with him.

Listen as God whispers, "No mess turns me back; no smell turns me off. I live to live in a life like yours." Every heart can be a manger. Every day can be a Christmas.

GROUP DISCUSSION (34 MINUTES)

Take a few minutes with your group members to discuss what you just watched.

1. What part of the teaching had the most impact on you?

Christmas Tree Traditions

2. Max said, "From childhood through adulthood, the Christmas tree is a rock that Christmas memories are built on." Use two or more of the following questions as prompts to describe your childhood Christmas tree traditions.

- Did your family usually have a Christmas tree every year or, like the story Max told, were there years you went without a tree?
- Did your family put up a fresh tree or an artificial tree? If a fresh tree, where did you get it? What did you look for in the tree you picked—a certain variety of tree, size, shape, fragrance, etc.?
- What color was your tree? Green, white, silver, etc.?
- How big was your tree? Too big for the room it was in, just about right, or small enough to sit on a table?
- What were your traditions around decorating the tree?
- What crowned your tree? A star, angel, other ornament, etc.?
- When did you typically put up and take down your tree each year?

3. Now consider some of the Christmas tree traditions and memories from your adult years.

- In what ways, if any, have your traditions changed since you were a child?

- What is your favorite part of having a Christmas tree each year? Share any stories that come to mind.

Christmas Is a Love Story

4. "The story of Christmas is the story of God's relentless love for us," Max said. "We might question his actions, decisions, or declarations. But because of Bethlehem, we can never question his unquenchable affection for us."

   - As you reflect on your relationship with God, when would you say you have been most aware and most certain of God's love for you?

   - Love is always a gift, and when it is offered we have the option to decline it or to accept it. To receive love when it is offered requires vulnerability—we have to *let* ourselves be loved. On the occasions when you have been most certain of God's love, how, specifically, did you *let God love you?* (If you find it helpful, you might consider the ways in which young children naturally let themselves be loved.)

   - Even though God's love is unceasing, we sometimes go through seasons when we either doubt it or struggle to let God love us. Perhaps our life resembles a stable—crude in spots, smelly in others—and we doubt God could love us in that condition, or we shrink back from letting him love us. What, if anything, has led you to doubt God's love for you? Or, when do you tend to shrink back from letting God love you?

5. Perhaps no image better symbolizes the love story of Christmas than a babe in the manger. Here is what we know about Jesus' first resting place on earth:

> She gave birth to her firstborn son. She wrapped him snugly in strips of cloth and laid him in a manger, because there was no lodging available for them (Luke 2:7 NLT).

There was nothing extraordinary about the manger; it was a humble feeding trough. It became the cradle for a king because it was available and because God chose it. And it wasn't a random choice. Throughout the Christmas story God consistently chose the small, the lowly, and the outcast.

God chose Bethlehem. God could have chosen a more prominent and distinguished city such as Jerusalem. Instead, he chose the little town of Bethlehem: "But you, Bethlehem Ephrathah, though you are small among the clans of Judah, out of you will come for me one who will be ruler over Israel" (Micah 5:2).

God chose Mary. God could have chosen the daughter of a king or the wife of an esteemed rabbi to be the mother of the Messiah. Instead, he chose an unknown and ordinary young woman who described herself as a "lowly servant girl" (Luke 1:48 NLT).

God chose the shepherds and the magi. God could have chosen to announce the Messiah's birth first to priests and rulers. Instead, he chose outcasts and outsiders (see Matthew 2:1–2; Luke 2:9–11). Shepherds were at the bottom of the social ladder in Palestinian life and the magi were both Gentiles and foreigners.

- The manger was humble, Bethlehem was small, Mary was lowly, the shepherds were outcasts, and the magi were outsiders. Two thousand years later, our familiarity with the Christmas story perhaps makes it difficult to grasp what radically unexpected choices these really were. To get a better understanding, consider what the contemporary equivalents of these choices might be.

Bethlehem manger: In your community, what is the smallest, humblest, most unexpected place a royal baby might be born?

Mary: Who is the most unknown, ordinary, or lowly servant of a young woman you can imagine giving birth to a royal baby?

Shepherds and magi: Who are the outcasts and out-siders that might be the first to hear God's royal birth announcement?

- God's choices were not only unexpected, they were also subversive. A subversive person engages in a systematic attempt to overthrow an established order by working secretly from within it. In what ways do you recognize the subversive nature of God's choices? How would you describe the "established order" God was working to overthrow?

- Although the characters in the Christmas story may or may not have known it at the time, God's unexpected and subversive choices were expressions of his limitless love. In what ways does this truth—that God's love is sometimes expressed in unexpected or subversive ways— challenge you? In what ways does it encourage you?

6. Max said, "In the manger God loves you, and through the cross he saves you. But has he taken you to his home? Not yet. He has work for you to do. He wants the world to see what God can do with his purchased possessions." Using the image of a Christmas tree, Max explained how God *prunes us*, *decorates us*, *surrounds us with grace*, and then *places us* to make a difference in the world. As you consider this season of your life, which aspect of this process do you identify with most? Place a check mark next to the statement that best describes your response.

□ *I am being pruned.* God is working on my character, helping me to address self-defeating habits of thought and behavior (see John 15:1–2).

□ *I am being decorated.* God is challenging me and helping me to grow in the fruits of the Spirit—love, joy, peace, forbearance, kindness, goodness, faithfulness, gentleness, and self-control (see Galatians 5:22–23).

□ *I am being surrounded with grace.* God is helping me to grow in grace. I am learning to rely on grace more and more—not just when I need forgiveness but for every moment throughout the day. This is what enables me to increasingly give gifts of grace to others (see 1 Peter 4:10; 2 Peter 3:18).

□ *I am being placed.* God knows me and has a purpose for me right where I am. He is helping me to love people and make a difference in the world through my everyday life (see Psalm 139:13–14, 16).

- Which statement do you identify with most? Share the reasons for your response.

- If it's true that God "wants the world to see what he can do with his purchased possessions," what might God want the world to see in you in this pruning/decorating/ gracing/placing season of your life? Use the following sentence starter: *Through me, God wants the world to see that he can. . . .*

Walking Together through Advent

7. Take a few moments to discuss what you've learned and experienced together throughout the *Because of Bethlehem* study.

- In session 1, you considered how Advent is primarily a season of preparation rather than celebration. In what ways, if any, has this perspective changed your experience of Advent or helped you to prepare spiritually for Christmas?

- Overall, how would you describe your experience of the weekly Advent practices? To what degree, if any, did they help you make room for Christ in your life and in your heart?

- What would you say is the most important thing you learned or experienced through your study and sharing together?

- How have you recognized God's work among you as a group?

INDIVIDUAL ACTIVITY: WHAT I WANT TO REMEMBER (2 MINUTES)

Complete this activity on your own.

1. Briefly review the outline and any notes you took.
2. In the space below, write down the most significant thing you gained in this session—from the teaching, activities, or discussions.

   What I want to remember from this session . . .

ADVENT PRACTICE

Before concluding, briefly preview the session 4 Advent practice, "Receive the Love of God." If your group is ongoing, allow time at your next gathering to talk about your experience of receiving and giving love. If this is your last group meeting, consider sharing your experiences with a friend or another member of the group one-on-one in the days ahead.

CLOSING PRAYER

Close your time together with prayer.

Advent Practice

RECEIVE THE LOVE OF GOD

A stable manger was Jesus' first dwelling place on earth. It was where he chose to begin his reign as Immanuel, God with us. Perhaps this is why the manger is sometimes used as a metaphor for the human heart—it is the humble place God loves so much he longs to make it his home. In his letter to the church at Ephesus, the apostle Paul takes up this image of the heart as Christ's home. And he describes the essential connection between Christ dwelling within us and our ability to both understand and experience the love of God.

> I pray that from his glorious, unlimited resources he will empower you with inner strength through his Spirit. Then Christ will make his home in your hearts as you trust in him. Your roots will grow down into God's love and keep you strong. And may you have the power to understand, as all

God's people should, how wide, how long, how high, and how deep his love is. May you experience the love of Christ, though it is too great to understand fully. Then you will be made complete with all the fullness of life and power that comes from God (Ephesians 3:16–19 NLT).

"The story of Christmas is the story of God's relentless love for us," Max writes. "Let him love you." As foundational as the love of God is to the Christian faith, many of us still struggle to truly receive it. In fact, says author Brennan Manning, "Christians find it easier to believe that God exists than that God loves them."[5] We lay the foundation for receiving God's love when we welcome Christ and allow him to be at home in our hearts. We continue to receive God's love when we trust him, spend time with him, and look expectantly each day for signs of his love. In this final week of Advent, you'll continue to prepare your heart for Christmas by seeking to recognize and receive God's love.

1. Look expectantly each day for signs of God's love for you. God's love is infinitely creative and, as the story of Christmas reveals, it often shows up in unexpected ways and places. In addition to looking for signs of God's love in experiences of natural beauty, in provision, protection, or consolation, look for signs of God's love in the places and people where you might least expect to find it. If you find it helpful to have a reminder, set a daily alert on your phone or laptop or write the following prayer on a Post-it note and place it where you will see it often: *Lord, how can I let you love me in this moment?*

2. Set aside fifteen minutes at the beginning or end of five days this week for prayerful reflection.

- Begin with a minute or two of silence, asking God to quiet your mind and your heart.
- Ask God to show you how he loves you—in this moment, as well as through your experiences in the day ahead. Immerse yourself in the praises of Psalm 103, which proclaims the many ways God demonstrates his love for us.[6] Ask God to help you recognize and receive the signs of his love for you throughout the day.
- Prayerfully reflect on your experiences of seeking and receiving God's love over the previous twenty-four hours.

    In what ways did God demonstrate his love for me?
    How did I let God love me?
    What did receiving God's love require of me?

    Use the space provided below or a journal to write down two or three observations as well as any impact receiving love had on your relationship with God.

- Close your time by expressing your love for God, focusing not only on his good gifts but also on who he is—loving, patient, good, holy, generous, faithful, etc.

3. At the end of the week, review your daily observations. What did you learn about God's love for you? In what ways, if any, did you experience God's love for you? Write your observations in the space provided or in a journal.

4. If your group is ongoing, bring your notes to the next group gathering. If your group has concluded, consider sharing your

experiences of receiving God's love with a friend or another
member of the group one-on-one in the coming days.

Day 1 Love Review

Day 2 Love Review

Day 3 Love Review

Day 4 Love Review

Day 5 Love Review

Week in Review

Briefly review your daily observations. What did you learn about God's love for you? In what ways, if any, did you experience God's love for you?

Notes

1. C. S. Lewis, *Letters of C. S. Lewis*, W. H. Lewis, ed. (New York: Harcourt, 1966, 1988), 383.
2. Ronald Rolheiser, "Being Ready for Christmas," ronrolheiser .com (December 22, 2014), accessed February 1, 2016.
3. Timothy Keller, *Counterfeit Gods* (New York: Dutton, 2009), 173.
4. N. T. Wright, *For All God's Worth* (Grand Rapids: Wm. B. Eerdmans, 1997), x.
5. Brennan Manning, *The Furious Longing of God* (Colorado Springs: David C. Cook, 2009), 76.
6. For additional passages about God's love, see Romans 5:1–8; Romans 8:31–39, and 1 John 4:7–21.

Also available by Max Lucado

BECAUSE OF BETHLEHEM

No one expected God to come to this earth the way he did. The One who made everything made himself nothing. He experienced hunger and thirst. He went through the normal stages of human development. He was taught to walk, stand, and wash his face. He was genuinely human. In the midst of your hectic Christmas season, Max Lucado urges you to remember these truths and rekindle your connection to the Christ of Christmas. To lay down your Christmas to do list and receive what Jesus has already done. And to heal your heartache by embracing the God who is always near you, always for you, and always in you.

Tools for Your Church and Small Group

Before Amen: A DVD Study

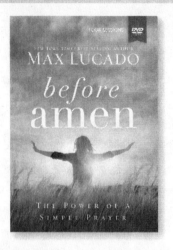

ISBN 978-0-529-12342-8
$21.99

Max Lucado leads this four-session study through his discovery of a simple tool for connecting with God each day. This study will help small group participants build their prayer life, calm the chaos of their world, and grow in Christ.

Before Amen Study Guide

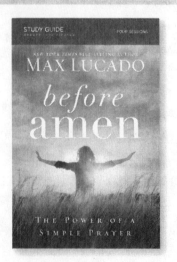

ISBN 978-0-529-12334-3
$9.99

This guide is filled with Scripture study, discussion questions, and practical ideas designed to help small-group members understand Jesus' teaching on prayer and how they can build prayer. An integral part of the *Before Amen* small-group study, it will help group members build prayer into their everyday lives.

More Tools for Your Church and Small Group

Before Amen Church Campaign Kit

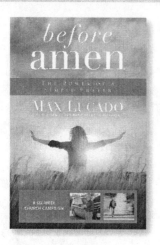

ISBN 978-0-529-12369-5
$49.99

The church campaign kit includes a four-session DVD study by Max Lucado; a study guide with discussion questions and video notes; the *Before Amen* trade book; a getting started guide; and access to a website with all the sermon resources churches need to launch and sustain a four-week *Before Amen* campaign.

Pocket Prayers: 40 Simple Prayers that Bring Peace and Rest

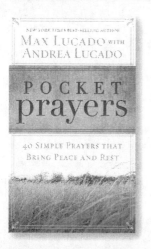

ISBN 978-0-7180-1404-9
$2.99

Includes forty pocket-sized prayers written specifically for times of uncertainty and turmoil. It's ideal for churches and ministries to use as an outreach tool.

Tools for your Church
and Small Group

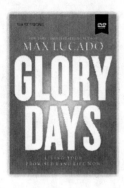

Glory Days: A DVD Study
ISBN: 978-0-7180-3603-4
$ 26.99

Max Lucado leads this six-session study of the book of Joshua and helps modern-day Christians live their Promised Land lives. This study will help small group participants leave fear and worry behind, overcome rejection, and deal with doubt through God's Word.

Glory Days Study Guide
ISBN: 978-0-7180-3597-6
$10.99

This guide is filled with Scripture study, discussion questions, and practical tools to help small-group members begin living their Promised Land lives now.

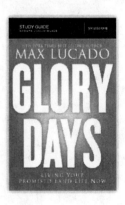

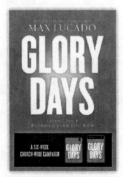

Glory Days: Church Campaign Kit
ISBN: 978-0-7180-3598-3
$59.99

The *Glory Days* Church Campaign Kit includes the six-session DVD study by Max Lucado; a study guide with discussion questions and video notes; the *Glory Days* trade book; a getting started guide; and access to all the resources a church needs to launch and sustain this six-week campaign.